I0080218

CROWN & CONFESSIONS Vol. 1

L.M. Wyandotte

L.M. WYANDOTTE
CROWN CONFESSIONS

Published by L.M. WYANDOTTE
Copyright © 2020 by L.M. WYANDOTTE
First Edition

PAPERBACK ISBN 978-0-578-70999-4

All rights reserved under International and Pan-American
Copyright Conventions. Manufactured in the United States.

No part of this publication may be reproduced, stored
in or introduced into a retrieval system, or transmitted in any
form or by any means (electronic, mechanical, photocopying,
recording or otherwise) without the prior written permission
of the publisher. This book is sold subject to the condition
that it shall not, by way of trade or otherwise, be lent, resold,
hired out, or otherwise circulated without the publisher's
prior written consent in any form of binding, cover,
or condition other than that in which it was published.

COVER & INTERIOR DESIGN: Leanne Padgett

PUBLISHING SUPPORT: TSPA The Self Publishing Agency Inc.

this book is dedicated to the most important people: those who have loved me, those who have hurt me, those who have helped me, and those who have experienced life with me. without all of you, this book would not have been possible. cheers.

also by L.M. Wyandotte:

crown confessions vol. 2

crown confessions vol. 3

instagram: @l.m.wyandotte

twitter: @lmwyandotte

30

i would love to make you
banana pancakes. not sure
i'll ever get the chance to.
just wish
i knew you when i was young.
maybe then i could cook for you.
a dream for another time.
i'll just put another penny in
the fountain.

50

to hold Her in my arms. an
eternal wish. i yearn for
the day it's granted. until
then i'll dream about a moon
dance. with Her.

75

all i want. like me. love me.
as is. accept me. flaws and all.
fat. funny. shy. loving. goofy.
caring. way i am. i'll be happy.

140

ever wake up and each day
is hell? it's like every
day is groundhog day.
where is my andie macdowell?

i'd relive everyday
for Her. i do know Her. but
not sure i'll get the chance
for that perfect day.

250

someone got to you. before i could.
before i knew you. that's why i wish
i knew you. when i was young. maybe i could
be him.

204

you. always in my memory.
tattooed on my body.
on my mind. in my eyes.
you're always there. shotgun.

146

people can change. that's something
someone says after they fucked up.
but they don't think about the
people they changed because of their
actions.

122

She winked. not sure what it
meant.
is that a sign?
is She interested in me?
or was that just Her contact?

oh hell.

69

you.
only you.
i wanna be with you.

but there are others around.
in my mind i can.
only be with you.
one day.

28

our flesh touches. our lips do
not. that's one of the rules.
this isn't love. it's love for
the moment. no thinking. no feelings,
except that one at the end.
when we've both gone. and want
the other back.

7

we were once great lovers.
but, we came to a fork and
both took the wrong path.
guess the other is to blame.

41

i think of Her when these words
come out. difficult not to. you
may not get it. but you don't
know Her like i do in my
head. She's uhmazing. funny.
beautiful, more than She thinks.
that laugh. gets me every
time. but nothing is better than
those eyes. THOSE eyes.

63

sometimes. just sometimes. you
don't wanna be around anyone.

even the ones that love you.
that's okay. just as long as
you go back to them.

127

not sure i could ever dig
a hole deep enough. deep
enough to hide this anger.
this hate. some is for people.
some is for something i can't
see. prolly will need an endless
supply of shovels. and whiskey.

78

i know. she is with me forever.
in spirit. i talk to her from time
to time. because i see her. each day.
it's why i smile. and cry.

230

it's simple. smile. that's it.
too easy to fuck it up.
just smile.

241

talk to me after you had a few.
then i'll know it's the real
you.

192

how are we in the same bed,
but sleep separated?

142

life sometimes turns to shit
and you can't do anything
about it.

move forward. fight. keep
going. don't know what else
to say. that's what i do.
if you know me it makes
sense. if not. now you
know.

87

alone.
that's where i'll be.
come find me.
we can hang out.
by ourselves.

52

it takes too much to be humble.
time is spent making the money
to then piss it away.

women. whiskey. weed.

what do you spend yours on?

maybe we can split the bill.

19

they say when you're going
through hell, don't stop.

but when your car breaks down,
you have to hitchhike with
strangers.

one time it might be the devil
driving. buckle up.

3

if your heart isn't in what you
do every day, then why are you
doing it?

46

i wanna go where you're only
mine. you know where. low lights.
just us two. i wanna hear only
your breath and heartbeat.
even if we're only together
once. some day.

116

not sure which is higher. my
tolerance for whiskey or
women. either way. i'm
planning for the future.
no need for a calendar.

160

don't tempt me with sex. i'm more
interested in your mind. your soul.
those will outlast your looks.
and those are more attractive. to me
at least.

208

stop. the tears don't.
stop. the whiskey doesn't.
stop. the thinking doesn't.
go. don't know how life does.

151

ants marching. in metal coffins.
looking forward to five
before sunrise. i blame
columbus.

218

a beautiful life. that's all
i wanted you to have.
i gave you as much as i could.
i would've given you my life
if i could. instead. mine is spent
thinking of yours.

249

i see you. just you don't see me.
at least not like that.
damn it.

110

i don't know when i'll see
her again.
hell.
heaven.
it'd be hell if i didn't.
it'd be heaven
but i'd have an earful for
god. either way.
why?

60

i can't move my hands any
faster. or slower.
i can, but want to speed up.

and slow down.

maybe i'll just lay on my back.
she'll figure it out.

otherwise, we're both fucked.
and not really.

18

if you faked your own death
would you go to your service?
i would. at least sign the book
and get some free snacks.

wonder who would show. hope
someone tells a joke.

80

the look on Her face. THAT wink.
no words were needed.
She said it all. but i still
love to hear Her speak.

176

don't look before you leap.
doesn't matter if the
safety net is there
or not. that'll take away
from your effort.

224

never felt this way. honestly.
can't describe it. but. i like it.
i love it. i have to have it.

152

so many words. so little
space. quality. not
quantity.

117

i can't think of a life
without Her. how the hell
would that happen? by this
point. i've come to expect
it. if it stops.
so will i. period.

77

all i can do is write about
her.
closest i'll get other than
a picture.
why? why her?
you don't have the answers?
then i don't want to hear
from you.

35

i feel bad for the people
that can't hold their liquor.
what a waste of money. maybe,
just stick to soda. and every
once in a while mix in a root
beer. spice things up. but
take it easy.
don't overdo it.

147

loyalty. so hard to find. and
because of that you think everyone
is bullshitting.
and you're right. they are.

248

you say those words.
the ones that make me think. that
i have a chance. with you. possibly.
maybe. i'll wait.

150

another late night.
whiskey. paper. typewriter.
may have a lady over. maybe.
either way. it's gonna be
a great night.

74

she lost it all. she was selfish.
we almost made it. nuclear couple.
but we didn't. you ever been shit on?
the stain is always there. you never
forget it. or the feeling when it
showed up.

21

that other woman. i want to be
with Her. but She has someone
else. i do too. but that bomb
has been ticking for a while.

not sure i'll feel the blast.

tick tock. tick tock.

124

what's the point of sober writing?

200

without you there's whiskey.
with you there's whiskey.
without whiskey there's no me.

65

free. that's how i feel
with Her. no judgement. me.

my body. my mind. all accepted.
as is. that's all i wanted.
maybe there'll be improvements.

if not. oh well.

15

does your lover need to love
you or love your body?
asking for myself.

and a friend.

205

these hands can't touch you. the
mind wants to. so does the heart. maybe
one day. that's all i can hope for.
that's all i look forward to.

70

is it bad i lost love?
it's not there.
it's starting somewhere else.

i didn't plant the seed.
just watering it.

24

how does one know when
they are an alcoholic?

asking for a friend. thanks.

193

these words don't exist.
not without Her existence.

99

She puts a smile on my face.
even though She doesn't see
it.
starts in the morning. usually
ends in the morning. i wonder
if i smile in my sleep. if so.
it's because of Her.

31

i tell the truth. i'll tell the
truther when the whiskey is in me.
don't listen if you don't want to hear
it. you might hear something you don't want
to. might be good advice.
what do i know? i've been
drinking.
cheers.

2

why be unhappy to make
someone else happy?
this ain't picking your best
friend for a pickup game.
you gotta play to win.
especially, if it affects your
life.

171

i lose my breathe at the sight of Her.
call me old fashioned. i want a
woman with intelligence. sense of
humor. personality. i'm attracted to
that before the body.
but nowadays, more effort is put
into the latter.

149

i can't forget. forget what she
did. i don't hold grudges.
i just don't forget.

71

have fun with the money.
it's just some paper.
it's not real. and what it buys
isn't real either.

you got love? loyalty? trust?
life?

you can't buy them.
i know.

40

i can't find some of my lps. i'm
not sure if i misplaced them
or if an ex took them.
i'm not sure which i'd miss more,
my records or whiskey.
can't enjoy one without the
other.
but i can enjoy both of those
without the ex.

183

bullshit. bullshit. bullshit.
my notes on what i saw, heard, and
thought
about what i saw and heard.
important stuff.

242

yawn. too early to finish.
so many words left untyped.
trying before sleep comes
for me.

91

few things bring tears like an
empty bottle. the other things
will bring even
more tears with an empty
bottle. at least i can stay
hydrated between store runs.

42

wonder what happens when she
finds out.
no more guessing. no more
secrets. hope She understands.

i know nothing will happen
but crazier things have happened.
i mean, look at that wall in
china.

1

most people won't understand
the choices you make, but
they're not living your life.
so, why feel bad if you don't
choose what they would've?

153

never cheated in a relationship.
didn't see the point.
either all or nothing. it's a
waste of time in the end.

209

i see her face.
i see her smile.
i see her brown eyes.
i saw her go.
i hope i see the first three
again.

247

share with me your heart.
your soul. your love.
i'll share mine with you.

92

i don't fear death. i fear life
after the deaths of others.
don't threaten me with
the punishment of death.
the scythe will not collect me.

49

to hear that laugh. even if i
don't cause it. instant joy.
like the first sip of whiskey.
eyes closed smile.

just that feeling on repeat.

22

a relationship is a beautiful
hell. the flames and the
feelings always burn. you
know they are there, but you
try to ignore the ones that
could hurt.

it's okay to get burned every
once in a while. reminds you
that you're alive.

144

i have this feeling. i'm
only creative when i'm
drunk. this poem proves
it. it's rubbish. but it
proves the theory.
exactly.

239

whiskey and words. both bring me pleasure.
both bring me pain. you bring both too.
but with a great smile.

133

but she
lost it. the place in my
heart.
by her own doing. she may
say i'm at fault. but it
was her that strayed.
not me.

54

too many people worry. it'll
work out.
if not, it wasn't meant to be.
either way.
you win.
as long as you win, that's all
that matters.

that's all you wanted in the
beginning, right?

11

how does life go on after the
most important one stops?

keep your answers to yourself.

143

that numb feeling. oh. it
feels so great. i can be
free. whatever i want. if
you don't believe me.
wait for the signs.
you'll be wrong. just
watch.

217

you. the only one i wanna
be with. not too much to ask.
may be complicated. but i've
fallen. and i want you to do the
same. see you when you're down here.

104

words. whiskey. the rest is
bullshit.

39

i forget about some of the
women i've been with. every now
and then a memory comes back to
me.
sometimes, i have a drink
because of the memory. other
times, i have more than one.

if one of you read this. write
me. we can meet and
drink about the past.

112

saw a unicorn. She showed me
magic. there were sparks.
a small fire. still burns.
no plans to extinguish it.

189

if you read these words. you're
looking into my soul.
you might not like what you see.
but hey. that's your problem.

243

i'd love to give you my warmth.
laying in bed. tangled.
no sun. no moon.
two hearts. one love.

102

roll. light. inhale. exhale. pour.
drink. type. repeat. life is
simple. don't fuck it up.

55

i can't help the feelings i get.
some are great, some are bad.

all are true. don't lie to
yourself.

above all, you know when you're
lying.

especially to yourself.

14

finished the drink. found
the bottle of whiskey
was dry and empty.
that's when the rest of the
care left me.
off to bed. the floor will do.

130

late nights. lots of ink.
few words. lots of thoughts.
at least i'm saving trees.
you're welcome.

211

the records spin.
i pound on the typewriter.
the phone rings. only the
first two are important.
the rest is rubbish.

101

i close my eyes. i can
see Hers. dark and deep. brown
canyons of peace. but. to see
in person. uhmazing. tranquility.

37

one more drink. one more bottle.
almost numbs the pain. that'll
be gone in the morning.
sunrise. pour a drink. repeat.

154

sometimes whiskey puts out the fire.
other times it fuels it.
but. it's always there.

226

one drink. the writing starts.
two drinks. you'll find a spot.
three drinks. you'll find her.
four drinks. you've given your heart to her.

120

to lie next to Her. see that
face. in the sunlight.
what a way to wake up.
before death shows his
lazy ass. that must be what
i see. if he doesn't show.
i won't complain.

38

dark hair. dark eyes. they are
sunshine in a gloomy world.
i can only get so close to them.
morals. etiquette. respect.
damn.

96

knock on the door. she stood
there with a smile and a bottle
of whiskey.
i said i'm glad to see you. she said
glad to see you too. i said i was
talking to the whiskey.

148

gone are the days. the ones when
she had my heart. now all she has
is my phone number. sometimes
i answer. sometimes i don't
it's a lose-lose.

214

wish you were here. with me.
so i could hear your voice.
so i could touch you.
wish i was there. with you.

111

fall in love. fall out of love.
what's the fuckin point?
may as well jerk off but stop
before going. same feeling.
just shorter lived.
at least i had a say in the decision.

6

those eyes.
THOSE eyes are my heaven and hell.
i'm only in purgatory when I
don't see them.

62

face down. empty glass.
empty bottle.
that's how i like to end
writing. if you don't know.

now you do.

93

i want to be wanted by Her.
not sure She wants the
same. from me. not sure i'll
ever know. at least i know
that.

158

up all night. thinking of her.
wonder what i did wrong.
one day i'll find out. hopefully.

210

you see the words.
you don't see the tears.
you don't see the pain.
you read the scars.

246

tell me. what's your fantasy?
prolly can't give it. but
i'll write you a poem.
you're welcome.

95

writing sober can cause as many
problems as speaking drunk. i do not
suggest doing either. drink. write.
speak. sobriety is for judges.

64

i made the list. Her top list.
the only list that matters.

not sure there is another.
i made it.
nothing further.

10

there is light at the end of
the tunnel. but you gotta
make sure you don't accidentally
make a u-turn in the dark.

174

gone are the days. the ones you
could have real true love.
each day you spend
dodging mines and randomly tossed
grenades.

244

waking up to you. what i dream right now.
but. reality allows me to at least
see you. small victories.

245

no clock. i lose track of how long
i'm with you. priceless.
wouldn't trade. ever.

94

money doesn't buy happiness. only
satisfaction.
usually temporary.
don't agree? what's the cost to bring
someone back to life? that's when you
really know. it's just paper. that's all.

47

full bottle of whiskey pairs
well with an empty chest.
then i'll get to typing.
she'll come up. as she usually
does. knock at the door
reminds me there is a temporary
replacement.
between her and the whiskey,
i'll forget about what's her
name. at least for the night.
then the sun will rise. oh well.

20

i don't know what's worse
being sober or the hangover.
when i drink that's not how i
think.

guess i'll pour a drink and
figure it out.
stand by.

177

you can drown your sorrows.
if you wear a snorkel mask.

206

why you? i ask everyday.
why not me? i ask everyday.
i want answers. every. damn. day.

100

i wonder if she's on the other
side.
upset. that she can't
play with me. i hope she
knows i miss her. every. day.
and will. until i can hold
her again.

57

i sometimes feel as though my
heart is missing.

it was taken when she left.
when she was taken.

however the hell you want
to say it.

32

the bed is cold. the other side
anyways. occasionally, a
woman keeps it warm, other
times it stays made. pros/cons
of having company.
kinda like having a foldout
couch. it's there when you
need it. not sure which i'm
comparing.
up to you.

9

one more breath, one more smile.
one more laugh, one more giggle.
one more look, to see those big
brown eyes.
that's all i want.
not too much to ask for.

125

i see your face. THAT FACE.
a sight i wish i could capture
for permanent memory. then.
i could be happy all the time?
but then. what if i could see
it all the time. in person.
what a tease.

179

i can melt you with words.
make you laugh. make you cry.
both. because you desire to. and neither
if there's love for you. but. if you
get all three. you get me. and you're
special. like a unicorn.

225

my heart is yours. you may never take it.
it will wait for forever. until you're
ready.

240

i've had sober conversations. unless
they're funny. they're overrated.

113

i don't need your body.
i need your soul. your trust.
that knowledge.
that you'll never fuck me over.
that's more sexy than you think
your body will ever be.

78

another bottle by myself.
guess i can't feel when
i'm full of whiskey. good.
i don't want to.
i want to drink. write. go
to sleep. see ya in the
morning.

45

it's not love if your heart isn't
in it. i lost both a long time ago.
probably why i don't feel either.

27

i can't tell you what the pain
is like. it's none of your
business. and i hope you never
experience it.

if you do, i feel sorry for you.

137

i'm not settling.
i'm moving on. i can't sink
with the ship. i feel there's a
lifeboat with my name on it.
land ho!

182

so much time is wasted
on others.
ones that are not worthy. i will
start billing people or
walk away when my interest drops.

136

i had few words with you. i
remember all were priceless.
priceless.

97

i often wonder what She is doing.
because. She's not with me.
i'm jealous of what
has Her attention. not just
because She has mine.
because She gets it.
She gets me.

66

the sad thing is. you never
run out of tears. you feel like
if you did, you'd stop being sad.
but. you won't. so.

cheer up.

44

when there's a knock at the
door, i'm not sure if it's a
woman or a man.
by woman i mean lover. by man
i mean a guy looking for his
girlfriend. it's happened
before. all i say is stay
or go. and i'm talking to both.
otherwise, you're putting in on
the light bill if you both stay.
and stay the hell out of my
whiskey.

164

her choices. her actions.
brought me joy. but also brought
me the worst feeling in my life.
well, 2nd worst. hope she's happy.
with silver.

212

cancer. FUCK IT.

L.M. WYANDOTTE

238

i'll pour you one. if you don't drink.
i'll have yours. you can keep me company.
how bout round two?

123

why is it so much trouble
to respond? not sure i can
continue the chase. i'm meant
for more than catch and release.
besides. i need a new
trophy case.

68

oh. those nights i worried.
about how we'd keep it
together. but now i'm not
worried.

prolly for the best we don't.
we're both better off.
without.

43

first thing in the morning i
think of is Her.
i wonder if She does the same.
i'm probably after what
music to listen to. maybe.
if not, i understand.
it's important to pick out
the music that starts the day.
otherwise, the day could go to
shit quickly.

17

keeping it together is for
rookies.
nowadays, you're doing your
best to not finish the day in
jail.

56

the bottle is dry.

so am i.
so are my eyes.

that is all.

114

show me hell. i'll look it in
the eyes. the face. smile.
and walk forward. i'll scare
the hell out of hell.
when you've been through
hell you show the devil a
passport and keep movin.

139

not sure She knows. not sure
She ever will.
all i can do is write about
Her. one day. She will know.
if not. i'll walk the earth.
writing as a hopeless
fool. like that idiot in
sleepless in seattle.

197

another birthday. i've cheated death
one more. death owes me. i'll
let him know when i'm ready.

222

her eyes. THOSE brown ones.
a forever heaven. i hope that's
where she is. she deserves it.
not the hell she lived in on
earth. i'm prepared for a talk with
god. if he shows.

235

tell me. one more time.
a compliment. to keep me on
the line. i already bit. just waiting
for you to reel me in.

181

She always keeps it light.
must be why She puts a smile on
my face.

203

remind me. why? why you? came into
my life. i know the answer.
happiness. i feel it
everyday.

156

i look forward to the weekend. more
people are themselves. honest.
loving. assholes. but at least they're
real.

88

to feel the touch of your hand.
a desire that seems impossible.
one day. one touch. one feeling.
bliss.

51

one too many drinks. is that
possible? sounds like a great
problem to have.
unless that means the
bottle is empty.
then it sounds like a horrible
problem.
i suggest sleeping it off. that's
tomorrow's problem.

4

you know, at the end of the day
most of the stuff you worry about
is just bullshit.

59

my head hurts. it's my forever
punishment.
i couldn't save her. no one
could. but, if no one could.

where was god?
taking a sick day.
unless you're him, i don't wanna
hear it.

86

those brown eyes. that smile.
they're both forever with me.

in misery. and in happiness.
i want one. but get the other.
not my choice. never will be.

118

i forgot about the woman.
the one that
caused all the pain.
not all of it. but
a hell of a lot. she was
a great lover. but she
loved others. she didn't
see it but that was where
the line was drawn.

159

my mind stays in an emotional prison.
serving a life sentence.
no chance of parole.

184

i see so many people that make me
want to drink. that's why i feel
better meeting people when i
drink. i'm more relaxed
and best-case scenario
i'll forget in the morning.

220

sometimes it's weird. i feel like
whiskey gives me the ability
to think of you without losing it.
emotions stay in check. other times
i'm a fuckin fire hydrant. it's a
coin flip. even i can't call it.

145

that's a wrap. goodnight.

109

of all things. Her face. simple
beauty. no changes. no makeup.
oh to place my hands on those
cheeks. to kiss those lips.
a forever dream. come true.
please.

67

a drink.
that's how it starts. that's how
it ends.

but the best happens in
between.

magic some way. a bit of sleight
of hand.

8

remember what you were going
to do when you grew up?
yep, shit happens.

oh well.

84

don't waste tears or time on
those that don't love you.
it'll make you feel worse.
from my experience.
it's none of your damn
business.

126

her eyes. they went for someone
else. i'll never forget it.
i lost half of my heart.
the other half a year later.
i don't expect it back.
just don't want
to feel like shit. at least
because of the first half.

165

a lonely poet. sits at his desk.
full of happiness. full
of anger. guess it's
half and half. at least the whiskey
glass is always full.

194

i only want one woman.
but they're never sure
they want to stay with me.
guess i'll keep looking.

213

i helped create her.
i didn't get to have a say
about her leaving.
because i would've said
stay here as long as you like.

166

you won't have a drinking problem
until you have gone through
hell. they give you a
complimentary bottle when you leave.

135

words for when there's whiskey.
night be day otherwise. happens
that way. might be more creative
with a drink in me. buy me one
and find out for yourself.

121

sober people have more
problems than drunks.
drunks just want
one thing. sober people need
too much. quit bitchin. have
a drink.

72

leave her alone. it will only
make it worse.
pain will continue.
tiny bits of suffering.

each call will make you think
of that moment.
when it all went to shit.
and she can't clean it up.

34

i don't need to hear the words.
just don't fuck me over. say
you're gonna be there. if you're
not, i'll assume you don't care
and i'll move on. you forget the
hell i've been through. i won't lose sleep.
i'll get a full eight. if i don't show
for you, i prolly got drunk. my bad.
i'll buy you some flowers and cook for you.

5

don't love if you don't want
your heart broken, just
stay on the porch.

25

alone. the best and worst way
to handle a situation.

at least you won't have to
share your whiskey. cheers.

48

it's a tough choice sometimes
between a woman and whiskey.
both will make me happy.
both will make me smile.
both may run out.
both will take my money.
but, only one will be there.
no. matter. what.
til the end.
that's true love.
cheers.

173

the thought. that we'd be
together. forever. was a nice
thought.
guess it's time for me to
think again.

195

Her curves. not ones to forget.
i can't. so much practice.

219

my life. very simple. all i want
is a faithful woman. some whiskey.
some paper. and a typewriter. and
love sprinkled throughout.

237

close the curtains.
i want you all night.
all morning.
just you. how you are.
but only for my eyes.

186

i don't know what's worse. seeing
Her and not being able to touch Her.
or knowing i'll never get
to be with Her.

155

your thought of pain differs from mine.
does it impact every part
of your day? if not. good for you.
you don't want in this club.

L.M. WYANDOTTE

115

what would it take? for Her
to really know. know how
i felt. book of
poems? a song? my ear?
hopefully just words.
cause i ain't got abs.

98

i envy hitchhikers. freedom.
courage. trust. it
takes more than
a thumb in the wind. not
knowing where you're going.
but to have hope you get to
where you want.
sounds like life.

138

am i an asshole because
i'm not sad?
my heart has been shot
for awhile. it's just now the
ship has finally sailed.
left the harbor. not sure of
the destination. but not
being in hell is a great start.

175

oh the thought i could still believe.
that she was faithful. oh well.
people still debate the moon landing.
at least i know the truth about
that one.

190

living without Her love.
like living without air.

221

be with me. accept me as is.
i will do the same to you.
love me. i'll love you.
plain and simple.

198

we go together. like a cheater and
a hopeless romantic. guess that's why
we're not together. anymore.

180

my heart skips a beat. when i see
Her. simple things.
She wouldn't see them.
hair. face. smile. eyes.
immediately lost. but found at the same
time. paradise.

163

my heart is a cup. and her love is whiskey.
it is very filling. sometimes it burns.

134

i can't get you back.
you're gone. i only have
you in pictures. no one will
know you as i do.
forever an angel. never did
anything wrong. sweet baby.

12

i can't imagine my life without
some people. i can't imagine
my life with new people.
i don't want to imagine my life
either way. imagine that.

236

the sun is setting.
soon the glass will be half full.
letters on the paper. emotions
for all to see. enjoy. but don't judge.

13

that way you look at me.
the way you bite your lip.
you make me think i could
have a chance with you.
but, then he walks in and takes
your hand.
better luck next time.

105

she says i drink too much. i
say i need a refill. she said
get it yourself. i asked
if she'd get it on her way
out. room is empty.
glass is full.

234

only thing that happens when i drink
too much is i write/type too much.
catch 22. gotta take the good
with the great.

16

she's gone. but she's everywhere
i go. she's the only reason i have
hope.

and none at all.

128

one more. just one more
drink.
then i'll go to bed. but until
then. i'm gonna enjoy this
second to last drink. suckers.

233

with each glass. the whiskey is easier.
burns less. or maybe that's my
soul tapping out.

23

i drank a beer for each of
her birthdays. i was supposed
to stop at 4 but now i've lost
count.

what comes after infinity?
that's the number i'm on.

196

i forget. how many drinks have
i had? i'll pour another and
figure it out.

81

empty ashtray. no whiskey.
no ink. no paper.
no fun.

232

the sun rises. the sun fades.
i dream of spending time
with you in between both.
oh what a dream.

33

not sure if it's the heels
or the black dress. or how her
hair is done. maybe it's because
it's up and i can see her neck
and the earrings are dangling.
nevertheless, she's sexy and
then she smiles. those beautiful
lips. just to kiss them once.
yep, i'll make the trade.

168

you can tell a lot about a person by
what they drink. and if they
won't. they already said too much.

107

you know what's worse than an
empty bed? an empty glass. when
both are empty. it's a bad night.
hopefully. the ashtray is full.
that means the typewriter worked.

231

i don't want time back.
i just want more time. with her.
if you can't do it.
don't sell me on your pipe
dream.

26

since the sun rose on that day,
my heart knew the end was near.
i was prepared for the passing
not the aftermath.
in my arms, i want to hold her
one last time.

141

Her lack of sleep worries me.
i don't have much either.
everyone has their own way. but
there's still that thought.
is this right? maybe.
oh well.

199

remind me. can you love two people
at the same time?

76

my eyes are filled. with tears
and anger. he let her die. if
not him. then he sure as hell
didn't save her.
what do you believe in? why?

161

i wonder if i'm more alive
when i sleep. the dreams are so
real. waiting for that one where
i get offered the red pill.

229

not sure She'll ever relate.
i don't need Her to. just
need Her to try. to even understand.
that's all.

103

i look forward to the moonlight.
that's when she visits.
i also look forward to the sunrise.
that's when she leaves. good day.

53

my ears are open. but i don't
listen when people talk. i try
to filter out the bullshit.
what makes it through is the
beginning and the end of the convo.

glad i paid attention.

L.M. W<small>YANDOTTE</small>

167

the sun is just a big fire.
but. when it goes out. we're all fucked.
just trying to give that generation
a heads up. here's your notice.

228

we're both playing with fire.
neither know the rules.
but both want to win.

29

can't stop thinking about her.
great times. shitty times. she
was there for all of them.
she caused the great times.
shitty times weren't her fault.
sadly, there's no one to blame.
wish there was. not
that it would help. oh well.

188

i can't touch your love.
but. i feel it.

223

would you mind? if just once. i hold
you. i would be gentle. i would enjoy
it more than you know. maybe a slow
dance? maybe a moon dance?

73

i can't wait. the day She
tells me She wants to be
with me.
time will stop. so will
my heart. what's left of
it. it'll be like the 4th.

202

empty bottle. empty glass.
stack of poems.
success.

108

the first time She spoke. frozen.
speechless. swoon might be the
best word. all apply.
heartstruck is more accurate.

191

glass half full of whiskey.
She fills the other half.

36

i forgot her name. but i
remember she loves to make love.

not sure you call it that if
you're not in love. that's what
she calls it.

i call it great pre/post drinking fun.
cheers.

227

the daily struggle to contain myself.
my hands. respectably. just to
touch your hand. face. waist to dance.
my three wishes. that quick.

90

when someone tells me to
look on the bright side. i wonder
if they mean the part of hell
that is most lit?

216

that one picture. the only one i
have. hair in the wind.
THAT smile. forever cherished.

132

unconditional. love.
you can have it. just don't
fuck me over. no one else.
me. you. that's it. not too
much to ask. forever is fine
by me. i'm loyal. just ask
the exes.

58

new bottle of whiskey.
new stack of paper.
same me.
same shit.
same problems.
different day.

187

there are a lot of women.
but not one has a soul like you.
will you share it with me?

79

i see Her. standing there in
the bright light. i extend
my hand. and we share a
dance. i'm happy. so is She.
all is right.

129

forever and a day. that's how
long this punishment will last.
others will come and go. so
will those that were there
before the punishment.
no worries. i'll be here.

61

it burns, where my heart was.
the other half ripped on another.
whole gone.
hole remains. half man.

172

i have no reason to lie.
not because of the whiskey.
because i don't care. what's
the worst that could happen?
you don't like me?
i'll still breathe.

215

not sure if it's the whiskey or
Her. one burns. the other soothes.
oh well. i like having both.

169

ever wonder what that ex from high school
is doing? yeah, me neither.

89

this pain is like a buoy
in a sea of whiskey. rain. shine.
always there. forever treading.

131

this bar pours drinks like
a toddler. careless and inaccurate.
i'm not here to talk. i'm here to drink.
pour. silence. i'll drink. bye.

207

i see the moon. i see the sun.
but not you. my days are
on repeat. i live on autopilot.

82

i said goodbye. she couldn't.
i said i love you. she couldn't
i stayed. she couldn't
i wanted her back. she couldn't.
she needed saving. i couldn't.

170

i can't blame you for the many
drinks i have daily. but if you
want the credit. you can have it.

106

worst part of being sober is
being sober. best part of being
drunk is not being sober. worst
of being drunk is all the ideas.
it's a win-win.

201

remember who we were? you. me.
at the beginning. perfect.
i see in the time capsules. the ones
i can hold. the ones i can't.

119

the sound of Her voice.
i hear verbal bliss.
jokes. information.
doesn't matter. open
ears. open heart. open mind.
happy face.

162

the day these words stop is the
day my breath does too.

185

you're only wasting time
when you throw away a clock.

85

i don't need someone to drink
with. besides. i only have one
glass. i don't need more germs.
keep that shit to yourself.

157

don't tell me you're sorry.
i don't want the burden
of judging your apology. make
it up by not fucking up.
again.

83

at the corner of lost and found.
want to ask directions. but.
everyone is as confused as me.
don't look up. he's not there.
don't look down. he's scared of
you. look in the mirror. ask
him for help.

About the author

L.M. Wyandotte is a prolific poet who writes on the theme of love and loss. He has been writing for many years, and considers his life as still being written.

crown confessions vol. 1 is his first book.

See more of L.M. Wyandotte's work at:

instagram: @l.m.wyandotte

twitter: @lmwyandotte

www.ingramcontent.com/pod-product-compliance
Lightning Source LLC
LaVergne TN
LVHW051359080426
835508LV00022B/2899